METAL
DETECTING
JOURNAL

_____

_____

DEDICATION

This Metal Detecting Journal Book is dedicated to all the etectorists out there who want to record their metal detecting adventures and document their findings in the process.

You are my inspiration for producing books and I'm honored to be a part of keeping all of your metal detecting notes and records organized.

This journal notebook will help you record the details of your metal detecting adventures.

Thoughtfully put together with these sections to record: Date, Start Time, Machine Used, Settings Used, Location, GPS, Items You Found, and Notes.

HOW TO USE THIS BOOK

The purpose of this book is to keep all of your metal detecting notes all in one place. It will help keep you organized.

This Metal Detecting Journal Book will allow you to accurately document every detail about your metal detecting adventures.

Here are examples of the prompts for you to fill in and write about your experience in this book:

1. Date

2. Start Time

3. Machine Used

4. Settings Used

5. Location

6. GPS

7. Items You Find

8. Notes

Date	Start time

| Machine used | |

| Settings used | |

| Location | |

Time	GPS	Item

| Notes | |

Date	Start time	
Machine used		
Settings used		
Location		

Time	GPS	Item

Notes

Date	Start time	
Machine used		
Settings used		
Location		

Time	GPS	Item

Notes

Date	Start time	
Machine used		
Settings used		
Location		

Time	GPS	Item

Notes

Date		Start time	
Machine used			
Settings used			
Location			

Time	GPS	Item

Notes

Date	Start time

Machine used

Settings used

Location

Time	GPS	Item

Notes

Date		Start time	
Machine used			
Settings used			
Location			

Time	GPS	Item

Notes

Date	Start time

Machine used

Settings used

Location

Time	GPS	Item

Notes

Date	Start time
Machine used	
Settings used	
Location	

Time	GPS	Item

Notes

Date		Start time	
Machine used			
Settings used			
Location			

Time	GPS	Item

Notes

Date	Start time
Machine used	
Settings used	
Location	

Time	GPS	Item

Notes

Date	Start time	
Machine used		
Settings used		
Location		

Time	GPS	Item

Notes

Date		Start time	
Machine used			
Settings used			
Location			

Time	GPS	Item

Notes

Date	Start time
Machine used	
Settings used	
Location	

Time	GPS	Item

Notes

Date	Start time

Machine used

Settings used

Location

Time	GPS	Item

Notes

Date	Start time
Machine used	
Settings used	
Location	

Time	GPS	Item

Notes

Date	Start time

Machine used

Settings used

Location

Time	GPS	Item

Notes

Date	Start time	
Machine used		
Settings used		
Location		
Time	GPS	Item
Notes		

Date	Start time

Machine used

Settings used

Location

Time	GPS	Item

Notes

Date	Start time	
Machine used		
Settings used		
Location		

Time	GPS	Item

Notes

Date	Start time
Machine used	
Settings used	
Location	

Time	GPS	Item

Notes

Date	Start time

| Machine used | |

| Settings used | |

| Location | |

Time	GPS	Item

Notes

Date	Start time

Machine used

Settings used

Location

Time	GPS	Item

Notes

Date	Start time	
Machine used		
Settings used		
Location		

Time	GPS	Item

Notes

Date		Start time	
Machine used			
Settings used			
Location			

Time	GPS	Item

Notes

Date	Start time	
Machine used		
Settings used		
Location		
Time	GPS	Item
Notes		

Date	Start time	

Machine used	

Settings used	

Location	

Time	GPS	Item

Notes

Date	Start time

Machine used

Settings used

Location

Time	GPS	Item

Notes

Date		Start time	
Machine used			
Settings used			
Location			

Time	GPS	Item

Notes

Date		Start time	
Machine used			
Settings used			
Location			

Time	GPS	Item

Notes

Date	Start time

Machine used

Settings used

Location

Time	GPS	Item

Notes

Date	Start time

Machine used

Settings used

Location

Time	GPS	Item

Notes

Date	Start time

Machine used

Settings used

Location

Time	GPS	Item

Notes

Date	Start time

Machine used

Settings used

Location

Time	GPS	Item

Notes

Date	Start time	
Machine used		
Settings used		
Location		

Time	GPS	Item

Notes

Date	Start time

Machine used

Settings used

Location

Time	GPS	Item

Notes

Date	Start time
Machine used	
Settings used	
Location	

Time	GPS	Item

Notes

Date	Start time
Machine used	
Settings used	
Location	

Time	GPS	Item

Notes

Date		Start time	
Machine used			
Settings used			
Location			

Time	GPS	Item

Notes

Date	Start time

Machine used

Settings used

Location

Time	GPS	Item

Notes

Date	Start time
Machine used	
Settings used	
Location	

Time	GPS	Item

Notes

Date	Start time

Machine used

Settings used

Location

Time	GPS	Item

Notes

Date		Start time	
Machine used			
Settings used			
Location			

Time	GPS	Item

Notes

Date	Start time
Machine used	
Settings used	
Location	

Time	GPS	Item

Notes

Date	Start time	
Machine used		
Settings used		
Location		

Time	GPS	Item

Notes

Date	Start time
Machine used	
Settings used	
Location	

Time	GPS	Item

Notes

Date	Start time
Machine used	
Settings used	
Location	

Time	GPS	Item

Notes

Date	Start time	
Machine used		
Settings used		
Location		

Time	GPS	Item

Notes

Date	Start time
Machine used	
Settings used	
Location	

Time	GPS	Item

Notes

Date	Start time	
Machine used		
Settings used		
Location		

Time	GPS	Item

Notes

Date	Start time

| Machine used | |

| Settings used | |

| Location | |

Time	GPS	Item

Notes

Date	Start time
Machine used	
Settings used	
Location	

Time	GPS	Item

Notes

Date		Start time	

Machine used

Settings used

Location

Time	GPS	Item

Notes

Date	Start time

Machine used

Settings used

Location

Time	GPS	Item

Notes

Date	Start time	
Machine used		
Settings used		
Location		

Time	GPS	Item

Notes

Date	Start time	
Machine used		
Settings used		
Location		

Time	GPS	Item

Notes

Date	Start time

Machine used

Settings used

Location

Time	GPS	Item

Notes

Date		Start time	

Machine used

Settings used

Location

Time	GPS	Item

Notes

Date	Start time

Machine used

Settings used

Location

Time	GPS	Item

Notes

Date		Start time	
Machine used			
Settings used			
Location			

Time	GPS	Item

Notes

Date		Start time	
Machine used			
Settings used			
Location			

Time	GPS	Item

Notes

Date	Start time	
Machine used		
Settings used		
Location		
Time	GPS	Item
Notes		

Date	Start time

Machine used

Settings used

Location

Time	GPS	Item

Notes

Date	Start time

Machine used

Settings used

Location

Time	GPS	Item

Notes

Date	Start time

Machine used

Settings used

Location

Time	GPS	Item

Notes

Date		Start time	
Machine used			
Settings used			
Location			

Time	GPS	Item

Notes

Date	Start time
Machine used	
Settings used	
Location	

Time	GPS	Item

Notes

Date	Start time
Machine used	
Settings used	
Location	

Time	GPS	Item

Notes

Date		Start time	
Machine used			
Settings used			
Location			

Time	GPS	Item

Notes

Date	Start time
Machine used	
Settings used	
Location	

Time	GPS	Item

Notes

Date		Start time	
Machine used			
Settings used			
Location			

Time	GPS	Item

Notes

Date	Start time	
Machine used		
Settings used		
Location		
Time	GPS	Item
Notes		

Date	Start time
Machine used	
Settings used	
Location	

Time	GPS	Item

Notes

Date		Start time	
Machine used			
Settings used			
Location			

Time	GPS	Item

Notes

Date		Start time	
Machine used			
Settings used			
Location			

Time	GPS	Item

Notes

Date	Start time
Machine used	
Settings used	
Location	

Time	GPS	Item

Notes

Date		Start time	
Machine used			
Settings used			
Location			

Time	GPS	Item

Notes

Date	Start time
Machine used	
Settings used	
Location	

Time	GPS	Item

Notes

Date	Start time
Machine used	
Settings used	
Location	

Time	GPS	Item

Notes

Date		Start time	

Machine used	

Settings used	

Location	

Time	GPS	Item

Notes		

Date	Start time

Machine used

Settings used

Location

Time	GPS	Item

Notes

Date	Start time
Machine used	
Settings used	
Location	

Time	GPS	Item

Notes

Date	Start time

Machine used

Settings used

Location

Time	GPS	Item

Notes

Date	Start time
Machine used	
Settings used	
Location	

Time	GPS	Item

Notes

Date		Start time	
Machine used			
Settings used			
Location			

Time	GPS	Item

Notes

Date	Start time

Machine used

Settings used

Location

Time	GPS	Item

Notes

Date		Start time	
Machine used			
Settings used			
Location			
Time	GPS		Item
Notes			

Date	Start time
Machine used	
Settings used	
Location	

Time	GPS	Item

Notes

Date		Start time	
Machine used			
Settings used			
Location			

Time	GPS	Item

Notes

Date	Start time
Machine used	
Settings used	
Location	

Time	GPS	Item

Notes

Date	Start time
Machine used	
Settings used	
Location	

Time	GPS	Item

Notes

Date	Start time

Machine used

Settings used

Location

Time	GPS	Item

Notes

Date		Start time
Machine used		
Settings used		
Location		

Time	GPS	Item

Notes

Date		Start time	
Machine used			
Settings used			
Location			

Time	GPS	Item

Notes

Date	Start time
Machine used	
Settings used	
Location	

Time	GPS	Item

Notes

Date	Start time
Machine used	
Settings used	
Location	

Time	GPS	Item

Notes

Date	Start time
Machine used	
Settings used	
Location	

Time	GPS	Item

Notes

www.ingramcontent.com/pod-product-compliance
Lightning Source LLC
Chambersburg PA
CBHW051033030426
42336CB00015B/2855